W9-BXN-276

AURORAS

A First Book

FRANKLIN WATTS
New York ■ Chicago ■ London ■ Toronto ■ Sydney

For my husband, Morrie,
with whom I came north to see the lights.

Cover photograph copyright © Jack Finch

Photographs copyright ©: Jack Finch: pp. 2, 8, 12, 37, 38, 56; North Wind Picture Archives: pp. 11, 16, 30; Photo Researchers, Inc./NASA/SS: p. 18; Geophysical Institute, University of Alaska: pp. 21 (Vic Hessler), 50 (Evelyn Trabant); Alaska Division of Tourism, Juneau, AK.: p. 23; John Caldwell, Institute for Space and Terrestrial Science, York University/NASA/ESA: p. 24; National Archives/Navy Department: p. 26; NASA: pp. 32, 34, 54; National Optical Astronomy Observatories: p. 48; Reuters/Bettmann: p. 53.

Library of Congress Cataloging-in-Publication Data

Walsh Shepherd, Donna.
Auroras : light shows in the night sky / Donna Walsh Shepherd.
p. cm. — (A First book)
Includes bibliographical references and index.
ISBN 0-531-20181-3
1. Auroras I. Title. II. Series.
QC971.S48 1995
538'.768—dc20 94-45562 CIP

Copyright © 1995 by Donna Walsh Shepherd
All rights reserved
Printed in the United States of America
6 5 4 3 2 1

CONTENTS

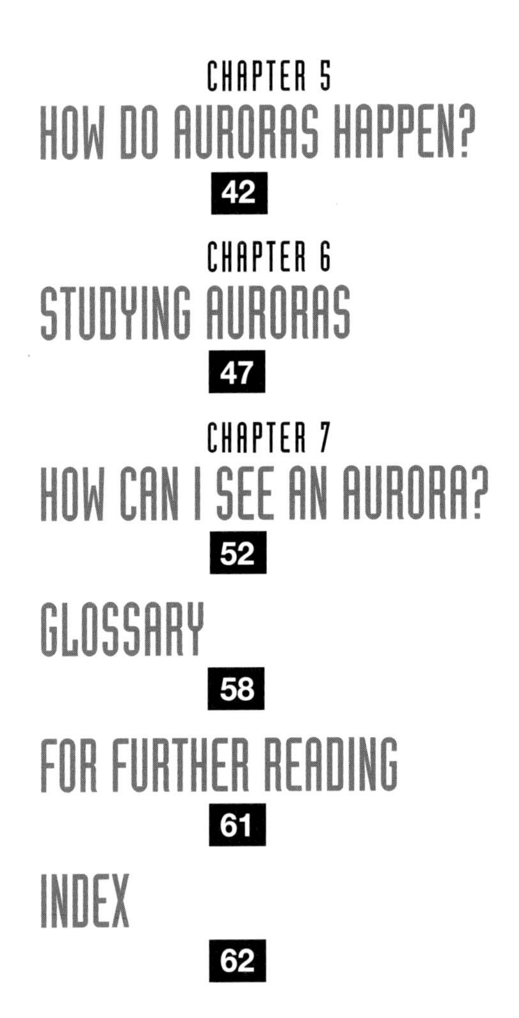

ACKNOWLEDGMENTS

Thanks to the many people who helped me with this book, especially Dr. Thomas H. Morse, professor of science at the University of Alaska in Anchorage; the Geophysical Institute at Poker Flat, Alaska; the others who read the manuscript; and Maurice Walsh, my father, who passed his excitement for nature on to his children—whom he readily awoke in the middle of the night to watch auroras.

Most auroras are greenish white.

WATCHING AURORAS

CHAPTER 1

On a crisp fall night, in a house not far from Fairbanks, Alaska, a young *Alaskan Native* boy was watching television. As sometimes happens on such nights, a message flashed at the bottom of the television screen: "Great *auroras* out tonight." Pulling on his parka, the boy stepped out into the dark night.

He gazed up at the Arctic sky. Above him, two pathways of greenish-white light swept across the sky from horizon to horizon. The paths of light changed course, bent, and swirled in a new direction. The meandering streams of light swooped, rippled, and washed against the darkness. As the boy watched, the lights began moving faster and became stronger. Then, the twin pathways grew together to form one wide band that rolled against the sky like a wave of brilliance on a dark ocean.

The boy remembered the stories his grandmother had told him about auroras, stories her grandmother had told her, stories that had been told in the Arctic almost as long as people had lived there. She explained that in long-ago times, people believed the sky was a solid dome covering the earth, with heaven just outside it. When people died, their spirits were trapped under the dome between heaven and earth. To free them, the spirit-god Raven and the spirits of their ancestors in heaven would dart down to earth and light torches along hidden pathways to the secret hole in the top of the dome. Finally, the trapped spirits could follow the shining aurora trail through the sky and escape from earth into heaven.

His grandmother also said that people used to think that auroras could rush down to earth to grab disobedient children, and if they touched you, you would surely die. Her ancestors believed shamans or magical people could call auroras to earth with a whistle. Only the shamans were safe from the wicked touch of an aurora.

Once, when the boy's grandmother was young, she and the other children in the village sneaked out into the dark on an auroral night. They stood in

Auroral displays have long fascinated the people of the North.

Auroras sometimes look like colorful curtains hanging in the sky.

an empty field under the auroras and whistled up, daring the auroras to come down and catch them. She never knew if they came, because at the first sign that the auroras might be moving downward, the children all ran to hide. The boy smiled at his grandmother's tales, knowing auroras never really touch the ground or chase people.

Just then, the solid pathway above the boy's head broke into bars like vertical blinds. The greenish auroral light swept across the length of the sky like *gossamer* blowing in a summer breeze. A red border grew along the bottom edge of this curtain of light. Like a magician's cloak, it seemed to swoop down to the earth and back up to the sky. The auroral curtain then folded in upon itself and became a ball of light rippling around the sky, dancing and swaying with the moon and stars. The auroras twirled, dipped, and soared again like neon lights that had escaped from their tubing and gone wild.

This sight reminded the boy of the old story about spirits playing soccer with a walrus skull in the sky; the ball of light was the walrus skull and the red border walrus blood. Finally, as if the skull had been kicked too hard, the ball of auroras exploded, shooting rays of colorful light in all directions.

The boy liked these legends, but he found the new scientific facts about auroras interesting too. He knew that scientists only recently discovered that the auroral lights come from great storms on the sun. Material from these storms rides on the solar winds to earth, and when the sun's material hits the earth's *atmosphere,* energy is released in the form of light and creates auroras.

Most of all, the boy liked just watching the lights. He watched for another hour, until the auroras faded and he could see stars showing through them. Soon the magic lights disappeared entirely, and the sky was as black as ever. The boy returned to his house and television until the next time the auroras came out to play across the sky.

WHAT ARE AURORAS?

The shimmering curtain of light that the young stargazer saw stretching across the northern sky was not unusual and not limited to the north. Auroras circle both the north and south *geomagnetic poles*, almost like shining halos. Although auroras are always there, hovering above the poles, they are not visible when they are thin or when the sky is light.

For thousands of years, people have watched the sky with amazement as it burst into auroral light and wondered if the lights were magic. Over time, people from all over the world have come up with their own explanations for the sky's auroral lights. In Asia, some thought the lights were two great dragons battling in the sky. Russian tales said that the spirits were lighting the way for the birth of a new child. For some Scandinavians, the presence of auroras in the sky indicated a change of luck—good luck would become bad, bad luck good. American Indian legends interpreted red

According to Roman mythology, Aurora (right), the goddess of dawn, opened the gates of heaven for the sun god Apollo (left) every morning. Auroras, named for that goddess, were originally thought to be a reflection of the sunrise.

auroras as the fires of enemies preparing for battle and white auroras as the torches of spirits fishing at night. New Zealand natives considered auroras the campfires of lost souls.

Other stories said that auroral displays existed to remind people of their creator or to announce the end of the world. As recently as fifty years ago, people believed that the lights were no more than reflections of sunlight or moonlight bouncing off the Arctic ice pack or off ice crystals floating in the atmosphere.

In 1619, the Italian astronomer Galileo named the glow he saw in the sky "Aurora," after the Roman goddess of the dawn. He mistakenly believed the eerie glow was a reflection of the coming dawn. Although he was wrong, the name stuck.

The lights around the North Pole are now called the aurora borealis (borealis means "of the north" in Latin). The ring of southern lights are the aurora australis (australis means "of the south" in Latin). The "dawn of the north" and "dawn of the south" are also called the northern lights and southern lights. Not many people live in areas where they can see southern auroras. It wasn't until 1773—when the English navigator Captain James Cook reported seeing them on a voyage in the South

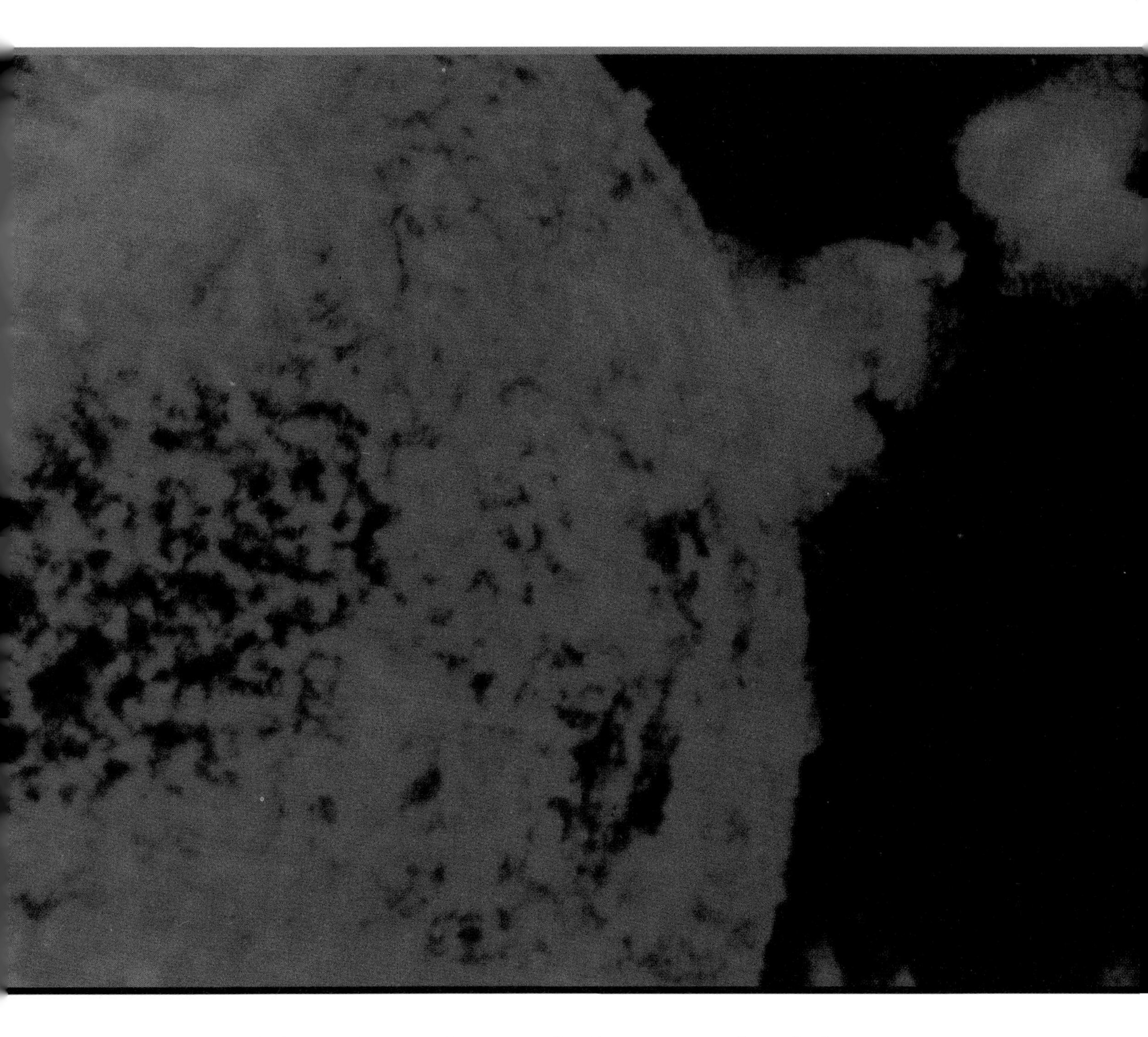

This color-enhanced photograph of the sun was taken by a rocket-borne camera during a solar flare.

Seas—that it became generally known that the South Pole had auroras.

In 1968, an airplane took off from Anchorage, Alaska. At the same time, another airplane took off from Christchurch, New Zealand. The two planes flew to equivalent altitudes above the North and South Poles and began to take photographs. These pictures, taken at the exact same moment, show the same designs, patterns, and movements of the auroras and proved what had long been suspected—not only do auroras come to both poles at the same time, they mirror each other. That is, a person in the north can see the same auroral designs that someone in the south can see, only reversed, as if seen in a mirror.

Although people used to believe all auroras were supernatural, they are as natural as the moon, the stars, the sun, and the air we breathe. In a way, they are part of the sun and the air. Auroras have their beginnings in storms on our sun. Dark areas on the sun are actually great storms called sunspots. These storms are accompanied by giant violent explosions on the surface of the sun. These explosions, called *solar flares*, shoot streams of sun *plasma* out into space. Tiny particles of hot sun plasma—made of *electrons*, *protons*, and ionized atoms—blow away from the sun in all directions. This is the *solar wind*.

When these sun particles travel toward earth they get caught in earth's *magnetic field*, which pulls them toward the north and south geomagnetic poles. As the electrons hit atoms in the earth's atmosphere, the atoms become electrically excited, causing the gases in the air to glow. The more electrons there are to excite the atoms, the brighter and stronger the auroras glow.

Although auroras can be any color, we see them most often as soft whitish green. This color comes when atoms of oxygen in the atmosphere are struck by electrons from the sun. Different gases glow different colors when exposed to an electrical charge. Sometimes there is a ribbon of red or purple on the lower edge of an aurora. This color comes from molecular nitrogen (two nitrogen atoms stuck together), which is closer to earth's surface. Nitrogen glows red, purple, or blue.

On rare occasions, the entire aurora will be brilliant red. This is caused when solar electrons strike high-altitude atomic oxygen (oxygen molecules that have separated into atoms). These deep-red auroras can often be the most dramatic auroras, producing a sky that appears to be filled with clouds of fire. In the early days of the Roman Empire, the emperor Tiberius Caesar saw the sky

An all-red aurora such as this one is rare.

turn red over a neighboring city. He quickly ordered his soldiers to help put out the fire, but when they arrived, there was no fire, just brilliant red auroras.

There is more to auroras than what we can see. Auroras include all three types of light that make up the light spectrum: *infrared, ultraviolet,* and *visible*. We can see only the visible light from auroras. Even then, our eyes aren't sensitive enough to see some of its colors, like blue, unless it is a very strong blue. Camera lenses, though, are larger in diameter than the human eye and are able to collect more light. The sensitivity of camera film allows time exposures that eventually "add up" enough light to photograph an aurora.

Sometimes during very strong displays, people say they can hear auroras swishing and crackling around the sky. These faint sounds are puzzling, because sound should not carry 50 miles (80 km) through the thin air. The best auroras are often seen in remote areas, far from *light pollution*. In such areas, there is usually less noise pollution, which makes it easier to hear faint sounds from any source.

Perhaps the noise is earthbound, coming from telephone or electrical lines that are affected by auroras. Auroras can send intense electrical currents to and through the ground. These currents

The changing magnetic fields that help create auroras also cause electrical currents that can corrode pipes, including the Alaskan pipeline.

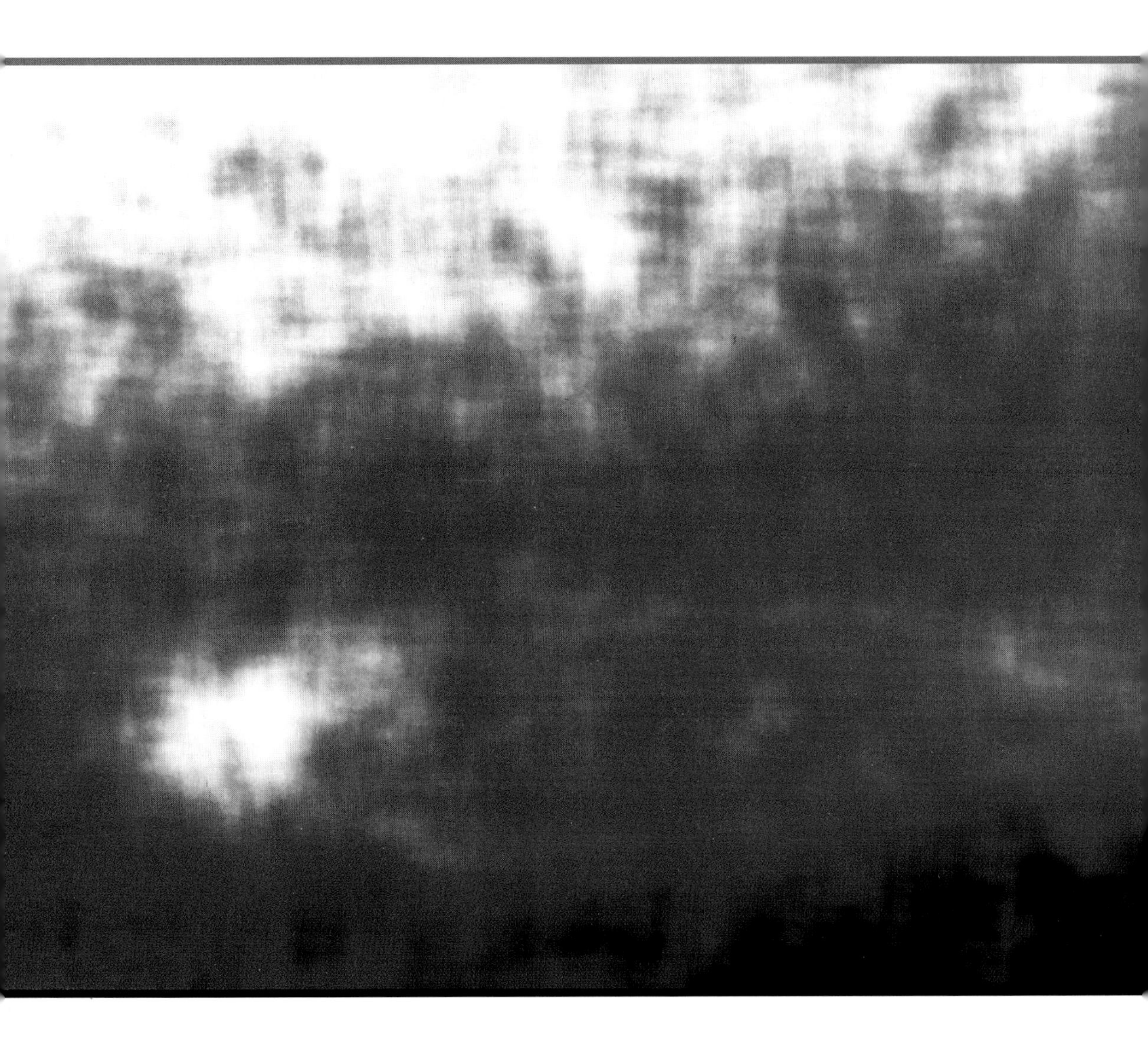

NASA's Hubble Space Telescope photographed this Jupiter aurora, which provided information about the planet's magnetic field.

may react with metal, such as pipelines, causing sparks or static, which people may hear. Or perhaps auroral sound is caused by something we don't yet understand.

We do understand that three things must be present for auroras to happen:

- 1 Electrically charged particles that come from the sun and travel to earth as the solar wind
- 2 A magnetic field to catch those particles
- 3 An atmosphere to glow when hit by the sun's particles

Earth is not the only planet that has auroras. Saturn, Uranus, and Jupiter, which have their own magnetic fields and atmospheres also have wonderfully colorful auroras.

Robert Peary stands with his dogs after a polar expedition.

WHERE ARE AURORAS FOUND?

CHAPTER 3

Long ago, people believed that the further north you traveled, the brighter the northern lights became. In 1909, American admiral Robert Peary set out to become the first person to travel to the North Pole. He was told to watch the northern lights to show if he was going in the right direction. The further north he went, the brighter they would become, shining the very brightest at the North Pole.

Peary began his journey heading north. Each day he took measurements of the sun and stars to guide him north, always straight north. Each night the auroras blazed brighter, reassuring him that his course was true. Then one night they didn't seem quite so bright. The next night they were even less

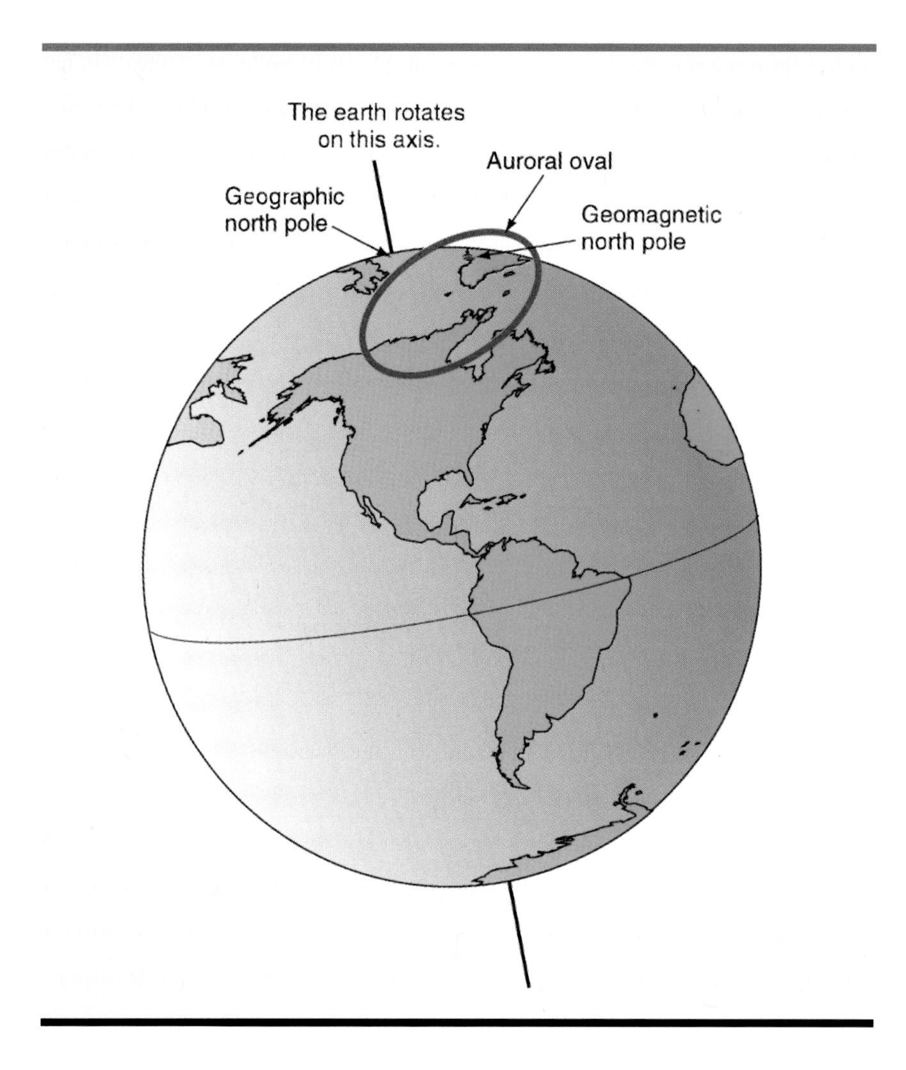

The geographic north pole (the northern end of the earth's axis) and the geomagnetic north pole, around which auroras usually circle, lie about 1,000 miles (1,609 km) apart.

bright. Peary's measurements showed his path was still true north. So why were the auroras fading away? He wrote his concerns about the disappearing northern lights in his journal.

What Peary didn't know, and what no one knew then, was that auroras are not always seen at the North Pole. They usually form a circle below it. And it is the geomagnetic pole—not the *geographic pole*, for which Peary was searching—that they circle. The north geomagnetic pole, near Etah, Greenland, is nearly 1,000 miles (1,609 km) south of the geographic north pole. While auroras shine an average of nearly 250 nights a year in the circle below the North Pole, they shine only 100 nights above the North Pole itself. Peary's recordings of the weakening auroras along with his careful measurements lead us to believe he probably did find the geographic north pole.

Although auroras are seen most often in the north, they are not exclusively a northern experience. Because auroras have been sighted in places far from the North Pole, words and stories about auroras exist in languages all over the world—from Inuit in the Arctic, to Cherokee in the state of Georgia, to Chinese in the Pacific, to Italian in the Mediterranean. After rare giant solar storms, auroras can appear almost to fill the sky and shine

In the North, auroras are most commonly seen in central Alaska, northern Canada, the southern tip of Greenland, Iceland, the northern coast of Norway, and the Arctic coast of Siberia. This is known as the auroral zone.

far south of the Arctic. In 1909, they shone over Singapore, only 100 miles (161 km) north of the equator. In 1989, they blazed so brightly over Mexico's Yucatan Peninsula, that people thought the jungle was on fire.

You can see auroras most often from the places on earth that form a ring around the polar regions called the *auroral ring*, or *auroral zone*. Both the north and south auroral rings are roughly 20° latitude from their geomagnetic poles toward the equator. The further north or south you go away from this ring, the less frequently you can see auroras.

In an average year, auroras shine 243 times over Fairbanks, Alaska, which lies in the heart of the auroral ring. But far south, at the lower edge of the auroral zone, perhaps as far south as Des Moines, Iowa, auroras still shine an average of five times a year. Once every ten years they shine above Mexico. Although there may be auroras in the sky, we aren't able to see them nearly that often in any of those places. Auroras aren't visible if they shine in daylight, and clouds frequently hide them at night. In summer, the northern night sky often isn't dark enough for an aurora to show up. In modern times light pollution may block our view.

The aurora australis, as seen from Discovery's *flight deck, is solid red high above the earth and greenish white closer to the earth.*

As auroras can almost fill the sky from pole to equator, they also can stretch 1,000 miles (1,609 km) across the sky from horizon to horizon within the auroral ring. They hang vertically in the sky like a bright curtain. Normally, the tops of these curtains are as high as 90 miles (145 km) above the earth. The bottoms are suspended about 50 miles (80 km) above the earth.

Although we don't notice it from earth, different-colored auroras have different heights in the sky. Solid red auroras are high in our atmosphere—usually from 120 to 300 miles (193 to 483 km) above the earth; especially tall ones can reach up to 600 miles (965 km) above the earth. The greenish-white auroras we see most frequently soar from 60 to 90 miles (97 to 145 km) above the earth. The red, purple, and blue auroras, born of nitrogen, reach from 40 to 80 miles (64 to 129 km) above the earth.

Forty miles (64 km) above the earth, at the bottom of the *ionosphere*—a layer of our atmosphere full of charged particles—is the closest the auroras ever come to the earth. Sometimes the combination of altitude and angle at which we see auroras make them look as if they are touching the ground just behind the trees or just over the next hill. Of course, they are no more there than the pot of gold is at the end of the rainbow.

Although we talk about auroras coming and going, in fact they maintain their place in the sky in an oval around the geomagnetic pole called the

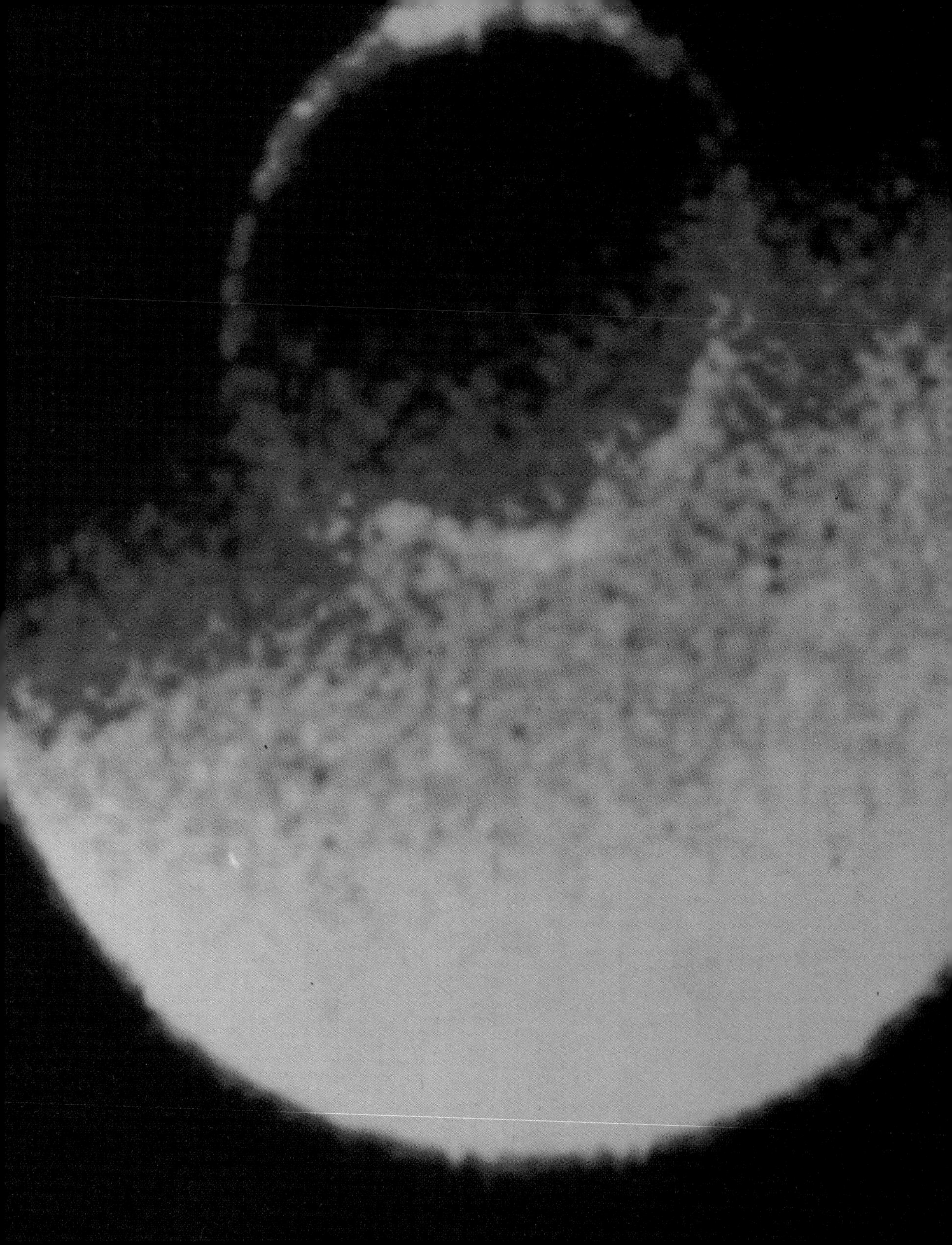

auroral oval. It is earth's rotating journey from day to night to day again that carries us under the span of auroras and makes it seem as if they are changing—first faint, then growing stronger, then very active, and finally fading away. In reality, we are earth travelers watching the cosmic scenery go by.

This is the first picture of the entire auroral oval taken from a satellite in space. The oval extends into the sunlit hemisphere of the earth.

TYPES OF AURORAS

Over the course of an evening, auroras change size, shape, color, and intensity. Some nights only one type of aurora will be visible. Other nights an aurora will go through many changes and look quite different by the end the evening. Among the types of auroras we might see are arcs, bands, *coronas*, and patchy and pulsating auroras. Usually auroras are seen for only an hour or two at a time before they fade away.

Auroral Arcs

Early in the evening, or on nights of minor electron activity, you might first see an auroral arc. These arcs look like shining trails through the dark night or paths across the sky. The arcs can

Auroras take many forms, including arcs, bands, and patches. This is a rayed band.

A corona is an optical illusion in which the auroral rays appear to converge to one point. It can be seen by looking directly up into the folds of a rayed band.

stretch for hundreds of miles around the auroral ring. They hang in the sky like screens of light. Sometimes the arcs shine only in patches and look like glowing clouds.

Rayed Bands

Later in the evening, if the electron activity becomes stronger, the pathways of light may break into vertical lines, or columns, called rays. These pathways of light rays, called rayed bands, are more intense in light, color, and movement than plain arcs. The columns of lights that make up the rayed bands travel along the lines of the magnetic field, which attracts the sun plasma to the polar regions.

Coronas

Sometimes sections of a rayed band fold over on themselves, much as drapes gather when pulled open. To see a corona, you must stand directly below the auroras and look straight up into the folds of the auroral curtain, which looks like a cone or ball of light overhead. Usually coronas have very high intensity light and movement. The cone rapidly turns, twists, and twirls in a brilliant explosion of light. Rays of light seem to shoot out from a central point, an illusion that comes from looking directly above and into the center of the auroras. Remember that things can appear to be different when seen from different places. When you look at a bicycle wheel from the side, for example, you can see the spokes and the axle. Look at that same bicycle wheel from the top, and you see something quite different.

Patchy and Pulsating Auroras

As the arcs, rayed bands, and coronas break apart and begin to fade, patches of activity often remain. Occasionally these auroral patches fade out and then flash back, creating a pulsating aurora. Finally, the auroras become little more than faint areas of light before they completely fade away.

Solid Red Auroras

On rare occasions, auroras appear as great red clouds filling the sky and are called high-altitude auroras. The strong winds high in our upper atmosphere blow the vertical bars of the auroras together and blur the lines of the auroras until they appear as a cloud.

If one type of aurora appears, other types may soon follow. Keep waiting and watching. Auroras may come at any time, and in any order. No matter how calm or active, dull or brilliant, patchy or sweeping, all auroras are exciting to see. When auroras fill the sky, we become spectators to the workings of the universe.

HOW DO AURORAS HAPPEN?

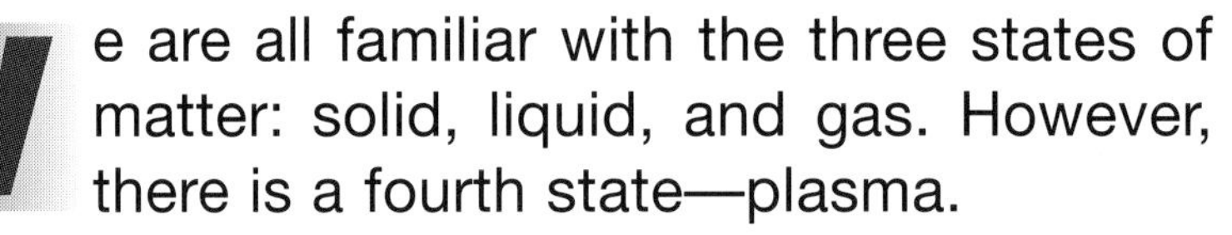

We are all familiar with the three states of matter: solid, liquid, and gas. However, there is a fourth state—plasma.

When you heat solid ice to 32°F (0°C), it becomes a liquid—water. Turn up the temperature to 212°F (100°C) and that liquid becomes steam, a gas. If you superheat that steam to tens of thousands of degrees, it causes the individual atoms of gas to break into pieces. An atom is the smallest part possible of an element that makes up the gas.

The heart of the atom is a nucleus made of protons and neutrons. Electrons orbit around the nucleus. A balanced atom has the same number of electrons as it has protons. When an atom is superheated, the outer electrons around the nucleus of the gas atom are driven away by the heat and drift off on their own. When this happens, the atom is thrown out of balance and becomes an electrical *ion*. The bits of broken atoms are plasma, the fourth state of matter. This plasma is a sea of charged particles, a soup of electrons, protons, neutrons, and atomic nuclei.

The sun is so hot that atoms are constantly breaking apart. As the sun rotates, that soup of atomic nuclei, protons, neutrons, and electrons flies off into space, much as a rotating lawn sprinkler sprays water in all directions. This constant stream of matter leaving the sun's surface is called the solar wind.

Sometimes great storms on the sun cause violent explosions. These explosions, or solar flares, send large bursts of plasma shooting out from the sun. Those sun particles, traveling as the solar wind toward earth, may be caught by the earth's magnetic field. Because of the earth's molten center, the earth acts like a giant magnet. Around the earth is a magnetic field that attracts charged particles from the solar wind. The particles travel in certain directions that follow the "lines of force" between the geomagnetic poles, just as paper clips are drawn to a magnet.

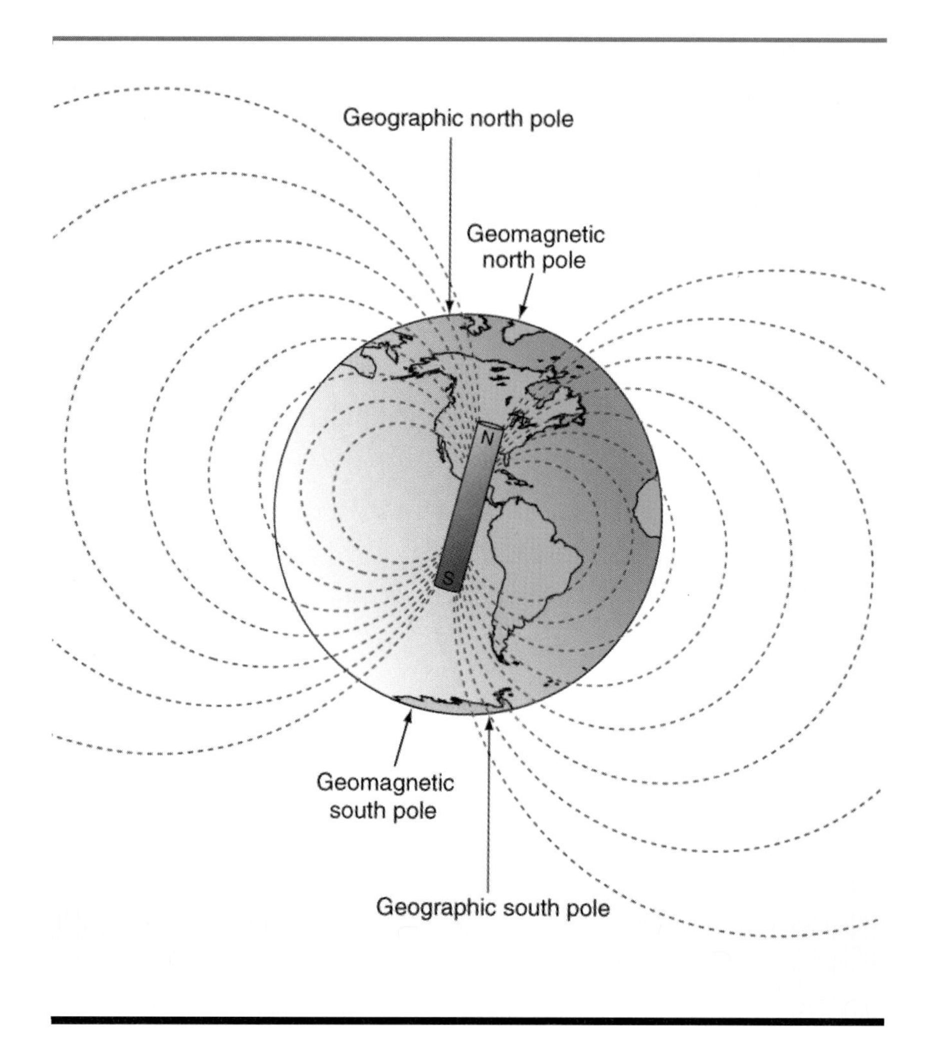

Similar to a large magnet, the earth has opposing magnetic poles that attract each other. That attraction between the poles creates magnetic field lines.

As the solar wind hits earth's magnetic field, it compresses the daylight side of the field, sweeps around the planet, and blows the nightside of earth's magnetic field out into a tail. Most of the electrons follow the magnetic lines to the nightside of the planet. There, they get caught by the lines of the magnetic field and spiral around these lines toward the geomagnetic poles. The electrons, far more than the other sun particles, cause auroras.

The electrons ride the magnetic field lines to a point above the poles in the ionosphere called the *mirror point*. They hit this point and, as if jumping on a trampoline, are sent bouncing back along the magnetic field lines to the opposite pole. They bounce back and forth on the magnetic field lines from the north pole to the south pole and back again. They travel these lines the length of our earth from pole to pole in three-fourths of a second.

When the electrons bump into atoms of the earth's atmosphere above the poles, they give the atom a momentary boost of energy. As the atom's new energy is released, the atom glows. The electron bounces from atom to atom, energizing each in turn, as if it were a pinball lighting up posts as it bounces around a pinball machine. The electron hits oxygen and nitrogen atoms all the way along a magnetic field line until it reaches earth's mirror point. Then the electron bounces back to the other pole to energize atoms of atmosphere there. This bouncing back and forth every three-fourths of a second causes the mirror images of the northern and southern auroras.

Finally, when an electron has lost much of its power, it stops bouncing and settles into earth's atmosphere. There, it blends in by rejoining the nucleus of a broken atom, thus coming full circle from the time it broke away from an atom in the sun's superheated environment.

STUDYING AURORAS

Because scientists keep watch for great storms on the sun's surface, we often know when to expect auroras. Although storms are always raging on the sun's surface, over an eleven-year cycle, the number and strength of these storms seems to peak. This increase in storms causes an increase in the frequency and strength of auroras.

When a solar storm sends flares shooting out toward earth, auroras will arrive in about three days. It takes the solar wind that long to travel the 90 million miles (145 million km) from the sun to the earth. Sunlight makes the trip in only eight minutes. A jet airliner would take more than twenty-one years to travel that same distance.

A solar scientist looks at an image of the sun directly projected onto a white table, making it easy to see sun flares.

Great auroral displays are more than just spectacular light shows. They can dramatically disrupt earth's communication systems. Powerful auroras have scrambled messages to and from communication satellites, knocked out telephone systems, blackened televisions, and interfered with radar and radio waves. Auroras have caused numerous mishaps, from the inconvenient to the serious. Once, during great solar storm activity, taxi drivers in Alaska got messages for drivers in New Jersey who were using the same radio frequency! In 1989, strong auroras blacked out large sections of eastern Canada. In one case, when a guided missile being tested was fired during powerful auroras, it received garbled instructions and began to chase the auroras around the sky before it was destroyed.

During World War II, just before the Japanese bombed Pearl Harbor, auroras shone over Washington, D.C. Before the lights were identified as auroras, people thought the Japanese had invented a new weapon of war. Later, auroras did play a part in the war, as they scrambled military communications on both sides. By watching for coming auroras, we can prepare for such disturbances in communication. After the war, the U.S. government established the Geophysical Institute in Fairbanks, Alaska, which runs the Poker Flat Research Range, to study auro-

To gather information about auroras, rockets are launched regularly from the Poker Flat Research Range, outside Fairbanks, Alaska. This is the 250th launch.

ras. Today, scientists from all over the world come to Poker Flat to cooperate in researching auroras.

There is another reason that we study auroras. Nearly 99 percent of the galaxies in our universe are made of plasma, the same kind of plasma that causes auroras. Plasma is not found anywhere on or near earth except in auroras. Understanding auroras may help unlock some of the secrets of our universe, such as how stars are born.

Because auroras are close enough to earth, scientists are able to shoot rockets through them to collect information. They usually carry out these missions on clear, dark nights in the fall and spring months, when auroras are shining brightly. The scientists measure the aurora's location and strength, the wind, and the rocket's predicted landing spot. Because the weather is so cold at Poker Flat, they pack the rocket in Styrofoam to insulate and protect the sensitive electronic equipment. When the rocket blasts off, the Styrofoam flies, bursts apart, and melts.

Some of the instruments in the rocket's nose cone send back radio information to Poker Flat, while others are examined after the nose cone, with its payload of information, is retrieved from the landing site. To help interpret this new information, scientists use computers, which have greatly assisted in our understanding of auroras.

HOW CAN I SEE AN AURORA?

Like the Alaskan Native boy living outside of Fairbanks, most people just enjoy watching the auroras. Unfortunately, predicting when and where good auroras will fill the sky is difficult. Unlike television, auroras have no program guides.

The best view of an aurora is from the heart of the auroral zone, far from the city lights that dull our view of auroral displays. In the Northern Hemisphere, the best place to see terrific auroras is outside Fairbanks, Alaska. In the Southern Hemisphere, auroras shine most often over the dark ocean off the coast of Antarctica. From the auroral zone, on fall and spring nights during the midnight hours, when the air is crisp and clear and

Northern Canada is an excellent place to observe and photograph auroras. Because the weather can be extremely cold, the equipment is often covered to keep it warm.

Taken from space at an altitude of 50 to 75 miles (80 to 120 km) above the earth, this photograph captures some of the colors and movement of an aurora.

the sky dark, chances are good you will see what our ancestors thought was the sky cracking open and white fire spilling out.

We are just ending a peak period of the eleven-year cycle of solar storms, which cause great auroras. The next year of peak solar storms is expected in 2002. The years before and after the peaks also provide excellent aurora viewing. Recently, however, scientists have noticed that auroras have been spectacular in "off" years and weak in "on" years and that we are straying from the eleven-year cycle.

Predicting when and where auroras will appear is difficult. They may come to any place, at any time. Maybe tonight or maybe tomorrow. Or maybe not this year at all. Perhaps next year they will come to where you are, no matter where you are. It is impossible to watch the sky all the time, waiting for auroras. Radio or television stations may announce when auroras come, or friends and neighbors may call. Sometimes, a brightness in the sky will turn into an active aurora.

We don't have to be earthbound to see auroras. Occasionally passengers in airplanes, especially on polar fights, see curtains of auroras high on the horizon, appearing as dawn spreading across the sky. Some of our best photos of auroras were

taken not from earth but by astronauts aboard the space shuttle as they flew over the aurora australis in 1991.

You can photograph auroras too. Try to set up away from city lights, because light pollution can wash out the auroral image. Use a tripod to keep the camera from moving and blurring the picture, and film that is very sensitive to light. If you can, keep the camera shutter open longer than normal, about 30 to 45 seconds for 400-speed film. Try to keep your camera and film warm if the weather is very cold.

As lovely as pictures of auroras are, looking at a photograph cannot compare with observing live auroras sweep across the sky and dance among the stars. Although we now know auroras are charged particles from the sun hitting our atmosphere, it is easy to understand why so long ago people used to think auroras were spirit magic. Even knowing the scientific explanation for auroras, it is hard to keep from wondering if somewhere in that night dance there aren't a few spirits left still spilling magic into the dark sky.

Blue and purple auroras wave in the night sky.

GLOSSARY

Alaskan Native — having ancestors who have lived in Alaska for ten thousand years or more, including the Eskimo, Aleut, Athabascan, Tlingit, and Haida people.

Atmosphere — the layers of gases that blanket the earth and some other planets.

Aurora — energy in the form of light released by gases high in the atmosphere after being hit by electrons from the sun. Most often occurs in the polar regions.

Auroral ring or zone — an oval-shaped ring of the earth's surface around the magnetic poles from which auroras are most likely to be seen.

Corona — the folds of an auroral curtain that, when seen directly overhead, appear to converge as a circle of light.

Electron — a part of an atom that orbits the nucleus; it is negatively charged.

Geographic pole — the northern-most and southernmost points of a globe through which the axis of rotation passes.

Geomagnetic pole — a point on the earth over which the magnetic field in the upper atmosphere points directly down.

Gossamer — a thin, filmy cloth.

Ion — an atom with one or more of its electrons missing.

Ionosphere — the upper region of our atmosphere about 30 miles (48 km) above the earth, full of charged particles.

Light (infrared, ultraviolet, or visible) — light moves in waves. Waves of different lengths create different kinds of light. Infrared light, not usually visible to the eye, has long waves. Ultraviolet light, also invisible, has short waves. (This light contains radiation and causes skin damage and cancers.) Visible light's wavelengths lie between the two.

Light pollution — the man-made light that blocks out fainter natural light, like light from an aurora, the stars, or the moon.

Magnetic field — an area where a magnetic attraction can be felt.

Mirror point — the point where an electron traveling on a magnetic field line reverses its direction.
Plasma — a mixture of ions and loose protons and electrons.

Proton — a part of an atom's nucleus. An atom needs the same number of protons and electrons to stay electrically balanced.

Solar flare — an eruption of storm activity on the sun.

Solar wind — a rush of plasma away from the sun.

FOR FURTHER READING

Charleston, Gordon. *Peary Reaches the North Pole.* New York: Dillon Press, 1993.

Daily, Robert. *The Sun.* New York: Franklin Watts, 1994.

Gallant, Roy A. *Rainbows, Mirages, and Sundogs: The Sky as a Source of Wonder.* New York: Macmillan, 1987.

Simon, Seymour. *Look to the Night Sky: An Introduction to Star Watching.* New York: Penguin Books, 1979.

Souza, Dorothy M. *Northern Lights: Nature in Action.* Minneapolis: Carolrhoda Books, 1993.

INDEX

Page numbers in *italics* indicate illustrations.

ABOUT THE AUTHOR

Donna Walsh Shepherd lives and writes in Anchorage, Alaska. She is married and has three sons. In addition to writing, she teaches literature and writing at the University of Alaska. She has seen auroral arcs stretching from horizon to horizon over Alaska, brilliant coronas exploding over the Yukon Territory of Canada, and solid-red auroral bars streaking down the Oregon sky. Although she knows the science behind auroras, she can't help but believe there must be at least a little magic to them as well.